x523.51 Boekh.P

Boekhoff, P. M. (Patti
  Marlene), 1957-
Meteors /

DATE DUE

OCT 0 2 2004	
FEB 0 7 2006	
JAN 2 4 2007	
APR 1 4 2007	

Eyes on the Sky

Meteors

by P.M. Boekhoff and Stuart A. Kallen

KIDHAVEN
PRESS™

THOMSON
GALE

San Diego • Detroit • New York • San Francisco • Cleveland
New Haven, Conn. • Waterville, Maine • London • Munich

© 2003 by KidHaven Press. KidHaven Press is an imprint of The Gale Group, Inc.,
a division of Thomson Learning, Inc.

KidHaven™ and Thomson Learning™ are trademarks used herein under license.

For more information, contact
KidHaven Press
27500 Drake Rd.
Farmington Hills, MI 48331-3535
Or you can visit our Internet site at http://www.gale.com

LIBRARY OF CONGRESS CATALOGING-IN-PUBLICATION DATA

Boekhoff, P.M. (Patti Marlene), 1957–
    Meteors / by P.M. Boekhoff and Stuart A. Kallen.
        p. cm.—(Eyes on the sky)
    Summary: Describes what meteors are and how they are formed, where they
come from, different types of meteors, and how they have been studied.
    Includes bibliographical references and index.
    ISBN 0-7377-1289-9 (lib. bdg. : alk. paper)
    1. Meteors—Juvenile literature. [1. Meteors.] I. Kallen, Stuart A., 1955– II. Title.
    QB741.5 .B64 2003
    523.5'1—dc21

2002000304

Printed in the United States of America

Table of Contents

1
Cosmic Dust

The word **meteor** comes from the ancient Greek word *meteoron*, meaning thing in the air. It is used to describe the streak of light produced as space dust and space rocks fall to Earth, creating trails of light across the sky. Sometimes meteors are called falling stars, but they are not stars at all. They are pieces of **comets** and planets that have traveled through the solar system for many years.

Cosmic Dust

Scientists think that meteors—and all other objects in space—began as cosmic dust formed when the system of planets that contains Earth was born 4.5 billion years ago. At that time, the sun first began to burn and glow, creating the center of the solar system. The heavier materials formed the inner planets: Mercury, Venus, Earth, and Mars. The newborn sun blew the lighter material, such as cosmic dust and gas, farther out into space.

Eventually the lightest materials became tightly pressed together to form the outer planets: Jupiter, Saturn, Uranus, and Neptune. Far

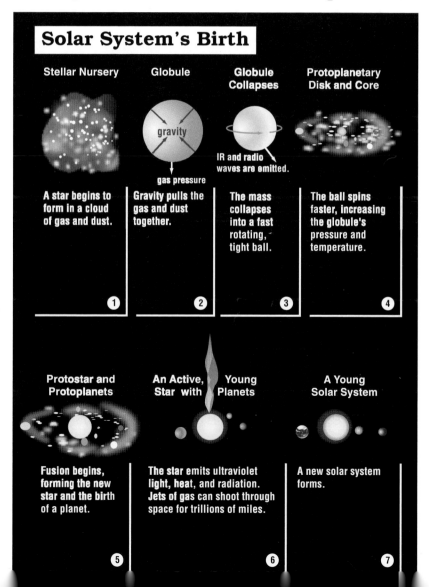

Solar System's Birth

Stellar Nursery — A star begins to form in a cloud of gas and dust. **1**

Globule — gravity / gas pressure — Gravity pulls the gas and dust together. **2**

Globule Collapses — IR and radio waves are emitted. — The mass collapses into a fast rotating, tight ball. **3**

Protoplanetary Disk and Core — The ball spins faster, increasing the globule's pressure and temperature. **4**

Protostar and Protoplanets — Fusion begins, forming the new star and the birth of a planet. **5**

An Active, Star with Young Planets — The star emits ultraviolet light, heat, and radiation. Jets of gas can shoot through space for trillions of miles. **6**

A Young Solar System — A new solar system forms. **7**

from the sun, these giant gas planets orbit in the cold, dark part of the solar system. Some of the gas and dust in the area far from the sun did not get pressed together into planets. Instead, it formed comets, which exist on the farthest edge of the solar system.

A comet is sometimes called a dirty snowball because it is a loosely packed ball of dust, ice, and frozen gas hurling through space. The snowball melts as the comet travels in a long path, called an **orbit**, that takes it from the coldest outer parts of the solar system to the warmest part, very close to the sun. At this time, some of the ice and gas is burned off, leaving a trail of loose dust in its orbit. This dust forms the comet's bright, glowing tail.

Meteor Dust

The comet's dust tail is made of small particles of rock and metal, which stay in the path of its orbit. This cosmic jet trail is called meteor dust. Sometimes a larger chunk of rock and metal is blown off the comet by the sun. This chunk of space rock is called a **meteoroid** or an **asteroid**.

An asteroid is a small, rocky, planetlike object that orbits around the sun. The largest asteroids are hundreds of miles wide. A meteoroid is like an asteroid, only smaller. Many meteoroids are about the size of a pebble or a pea,

A researcher holds a meteorite in front of a light, revealing yellow olivine deposits.

while meteor dust is about the size of a grain of sand or smaller.

A Meteor Is Born

When Earth passes through the orbit of a comet, some of the meteor dust and meteoroids enter Earth's atmosphere, which is a thick blanket of gases that surrounds and protects the planet. There are so many particles floating

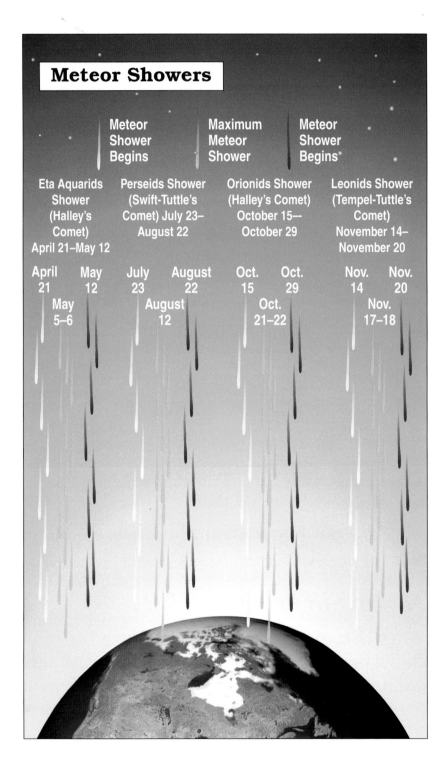

Meteor Showers

Meteor Shower Begins		Maximum Meteor Shower		Meteor Shower Begins*	
Eta Aquarids Shower (Halley's Comet) April 21–May 12		Perseids Shower (Swift-Tuttle's Comet) July 23– August 22		Orionids Shower (Halley's Comet) October 15– October 29		Leonids Shower (Tempel-Tuttle's Comet) November 14– November 20
April 21	May 12	July 23	August 22	Oct. 15	Oct. 29	Nov. 14	Nov. 20
May 5–6		August 12		Oct. 21–22		Nov. 17–18	

in space that Earth gains about twenty-five thousand tons of material—the same weight as twelve elephants—a day from millions of grains of meteor dust that enter the atmosphere.

A meteoroid might fall at a speed of about 150,000 miles an hour. As it falls, a meteoroid rubs against the dust, gases, and other tiny specks of material that make up the atmosphere. The rubbing, called **friction**, causes the atmosphere to heat up to temperatures as high as 4,000°F. (This friction is the same process that starts a fire by rubbing two sticks together.)

The atmosphere burns and glows, leaving a cloud of white-hot gases trailing behind. This trail of light is called a meteor. A meteoroid the size of a walnut can create a meteor about one thousand feet long.

Meteor Showers

When many meteors burn up in the air and make a light show above Earth, it is called a meteor shower. Some meteor showers come from the path of known comets, and some are the remains of unknown comets. Meteor showers are named after the stars in the area of the sky where they appear. For instance, the Orionids meteor shower rains out of the sky near the **constellation** Orion.

Every year in August, when Earth passes through the orbit of the comet Swift-Tuttle, the

Perseid meteor shower creates bright "shooting stars" across the sky. Halley's comet has two meteor showers: the Eta Aquarids in May and the Orionids in October. The Leonid meteors orbit with the comet Tempel-Tuttle, and appear as the Leonid meteor showers in November.

When a huge number of meteors appear in the sky, it is called a meteor storm, with as many as one hundred thousand meteors an hour streaking through Earth's atmosphere throughout several nights.

Every thirty-three years or so, the Leonid meteor shower becomes a meteor storm, and the display in November 2001 amazed those

Leonid meteors shower Earth in mid-November as the planet passes through comet Tempel-Tuttle's tail.

who saw it. Hundreds of meteors burst in the night sky every hour, sometimes several at a time. Even in the city, where the lights usually make meteor viewing impossible, the spectacular show lasted until dawn.

The meteors looked like a fireworks display on the 4th of July, leaving trails of bright dust that stayed in the sky for several minutes. Some had glowing green tails or orange heads with white trails. Observers even reported seeing fireballs light up the sky as they burst in the air. And while most meteor showers require patient viewing to see even one meteor, on this special night in 2001 the sky lit up with a wonderful light show that could be seen with just a few minutes of viewing.

Geminids

In mid-December there is a beautiful, bright meteor shower called the Geminids. Unlike most meteor showers, the Geminids are caused by the dust from asteroid 3200 Phaeton instead of comet dust. Some scientists think that Phaeton may once have been a comet, but now it is an asteroid in a cometlike orbit.

When asteroid Phaeton passes close to the sun, some of its dust blows off to create meteor dust. This dust is heavier, denser, and contains more metal than comet dust, which makes the Geminid meteors blaze with blue and other

Bright blue and white Geminid meteors streak across the sky above Arizona's Barringer meteor crater.

colors. Most meteor showers do not start until after midnight, but the Geminids can be seen even earlier.

Although the Geminid, Perseid, and Leonid meteor showers are well known among star watchers, falling stars may be seen on almost any night. Whether they come from asteroids or comets, meteors are all made of star dust, blown off the sun many years before Earth was formed.

2
Carbon Meteorites

Meteors that do not burn up in Earth's atmosphere but survive to land on the ground are called **meteorites**. Many meteorites come from the main asteroid belt, a doughnut-shaped area near Jupiter where millions of asteroids orbit the sun. These asteroids sometimes bump into each other, chipping off pieces to make little asteroids, called meteoroids. The meteoroids stay in orbit near their parent body (the asteroid they came from).

The main asteroid belt is sometimes called a mini–solar system, with Jupiter taking the place of the sun, and asteroids acting as miniplanets. Jupiter has a strong gravitational pull because it is so large. In fact, Jupiter is the largest planet in the solar system and is surrounded by an

An artist illustrates the main asteroid belt orbiting the sun (center) near Jupiter (top right).

atmosphere filled with lightning storms. Some scientists believe there is no solid ground under the enormous storm systems of Jupiter, only a slushy liquid center.

Many odd objects circle around Jupiter's mini–solar system. Seventeen moons and three rings, probably made of small meteoroids, circle the planet. Some of Jupiter's moons are icy comets, some are rocky like asteroids, and some are round with a cratered volcanic surface, like little planets. Astronomers believe that the gravity of the giant planet holds all these objects in the main asteroid belt, protecting Mercury, Venus, Earth, and Mars (the inner planets) from wandering asteroids.

There are gaps in the asteroid belt where no objects may orbit. If an asteroid wanders into this gap, Jupiter's gravity will either pull it in to its fiery atmosphere or push it out of its orbit. If it is pushed out, it may cross the paths of the inner planets as it heads toward the sun. Then there is a chance the asteroid may enter Earth's orbit and become a meteor.

Cometlike Asteroids

More than 75 percent of known asteroids in the main asteroid belt are very cometlike. They are called carbonaceous chondrites, or carbon-type asteroids. They are black and crumbly because they contain carbon, like soot or pencil lead. (Carbon is the basis for all life forms on Earth.) These objects also contain saltwater, like Earth's oceans, and complex carbon compounds, called amino acids, like those found in

A crumbly, carbonlike asteroid believed to have come from Mars.

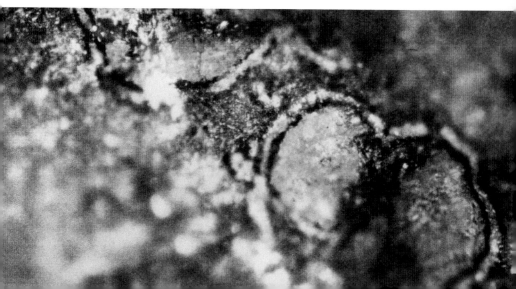

all living things. And the mineral grains they contain are even older than the solar system—pieces of dust that formed long ago around distant stars.

Comets and carbon asteroids are alike in almost every way, with one exception: Comets usually contain more ice water, and asteroids usually do not grow tails. But some carbon asteroids have large amounts of ice inside, and some have been known to grow small tails for short periods of time. For example, asteroid 1979 OW7 surprised astronomers by growing a tail for a few weeks in 1996.

Astronomers think it might have been a comet that became stuck in the main asteroid belt. There the comet gathered carbon dust that smothered the gas and ice. Once it became an asteroid, it may have collided with another asteroid in the main belt. A collision could break the asteroid open, exposing the gases and liquids inside. Once exposed, the gases and liquids could heat up and form a tail like a comet.

Baby Planets

These cometlike asteroids and asteroid-like comets are baby planets that are still in the process of changing and forming. Astronomers have seen both comets and asteroids that appear to have been fused together or split in half

Ejected from the asteroid belt, a meteorite crashes into Earth on its way toward the sun.

when they bump into each other. If they are bumped hard, they may be **ejected** from the asteroid belt.

When they are bumped out of the main asteroid belt, they usually crash into the sun. Some of them hit the inner planets on their journey toward the sun. When they fall to Earth, they are called carbonaceous chondrite meteorites. Their parent bodies may be asteroid-like comets and cometlike asteroids that do not fully burn before hitting Earth.

If a meteorite falls unseen and someone finds it later, it is called a meteorite find. If someone sees it come down, it is called a meteorite fall. Carbon meteorites are fragile and crumbly and will often disappear unless someone sees them fall and gathers them up very quickly after hitting the ground. If they get wet, they melt into a black, tarry sludge and sink into the earth.

Meteorite Falls

On September 28, 1969, a carbon meteorite fell over Murchison, Australia. More than two hundred pounds of this meteorite have been found. Because the Murchison meteorite was about 12 percent water, scientists think it came from a comet. More than ninety-two different amino acids, the building blocks of all life on Earth, have been found within the Murchison meteorite. Nineteen of these amino acids are found on Earth. The rest of the amino acids are not known to exist on Earth.

Water was also found in a carbon meteorite that burned through the sky and fell close to seven children playing basketball in Monahans, Texas, on March 22, 1998. When it landed, the meteorite was about the size of a soccer ball, glowing white and still warm. Soon, it iced over as the warmth from its journey through Earth's atmosphere wore off.

The children sold a large piece for $23,000, while a smaller piece was sent to the laboratories of NASA's Johnson Space Center in Houston. There, scientists cracked the meteorite open and found tiny bubbles of water trapped in

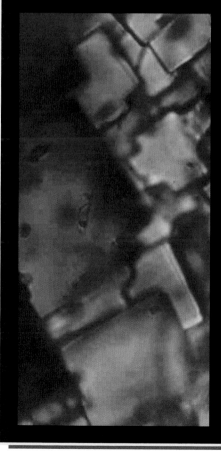

A carbon meteorite found in Monahans, Texas (top), contained water droplets trapped in crystals of rock salt.

purple and blue crystals of nearly pure rock salt. It was exactly like sea salt or ordinary table salt, but it had turned purple and blue while traveling through space for billions of years.

Astronomers have long thought that the water that flowed through asteroids and comets formed when the solar system was born. Carbon-type meteorites, such as those found in Murchison and Monahans, are thought to be made of some of the most basic ingredients from the early solar system. This means that the water in the crystals could be 4.5 billion years old—older than Earth!

Yukon Fall

On the morning of January 18, 2000, a large number of very rare, very fragile space rocks fell on a frozen lake in Canada. Witnesses saw a long shooting star of many colors that lasted for about fifteen seconds.

As the meteor exploded, two loud booms were heard throughout Alaska and northwestern Canada. Two flares lit up the sky, and the brighter of the two glowed with a blue-green light ten times as bright as daylight. The meteorite made sizzling sounds as it broke up into pieces. Witnesses smelled sulfur and hot burning rocks. Two dust trails stayed in the sky for a few hours after the fall.

Samples of meteors found in Mexico, Canada, and Australia contain the basic building blocks of life.

Scientists believe the carbon meteorite was about the size of a school bus, but most of it broke apart and burned up in the atmosphere before landing. Hundreds of small, dark meteorites shattered on the frozen lake or landed in the soft snow. The pieces that were found were between the sizes of a charcoal briquette and a fingernail.

There was no major meteor shower that day. The meteorites were dust particles that had bubbled off the surface of a comet passing close to the sun. Carbon meteorites are rare because they are fragile and disappear into the earth soon after they fall. They contain many odd ingredients, such as tiny nanodiamonds created when the carbon is crushed and hardened by collisions. These ancient meteorites help scientists understand the materials that went into making up Earth, the moon, and the sun.

3
Stony Meteorites

When meteors fall to Earth as meteorites, they bring cosmic materials down with them. Comet dust brings the lightest materials, such as gases and tiny bits of dust, which surround Earth to make up its atmosphere. Carbon meteorites contain the slightly heavier materials that cover the surface of Earth. These include seawater and carbon compounds such as amino acids, the basic building blocks for all the plants and animals and some of the rocks and minerals that make up Earth.

Under these layers of earth, a heavier layer of volcanic rock and sand covers the entire surface of the planet, including seafloors. Large reddish colored stony asteroids are small planets that are also covered in these heavier volcanic

A reddish meteorite reveals a solid iron core beneath crumbling outer layers.

materials. As they age, these large asteroids are heated and separated into layers, with the heaviest materials sinking to the center, or core. The core of a large stony asteroid contains iron and other metals, just like Earth and the other inner planets.

There are many such volcanic asteroids, and a few inner planets, that may be the source of stony meteorites that fall to Earth. By studying the color and brightness of asteroids and collecting rock samples from nearby planets, scientists have discovered that some stony meteorites are pieces of the moon, Mars, and the asteroid Vesta.

Vesta

Vesta is the third-largest asteroid in the main asteroid belt and also the brightest. It is classified by scientists as both a large asteroid and a small planet. Like Earth, Vesta is made of layers of rock. It has a hot metal center, called a core, and a middle layer, called the mantle, which is made of a green volcanic rock called olivine. The outer layer, or crust, is made of a hard, dark, shiny melted lava called basalt. These are the same as the materials that make up Earth.

Part of Vesta's crust was knocked away long ago, leaving a huge, bowl-shaped hole almost as big as the planet. (Earth also has such a **basin**, called the Pacific Basin, which is filled with the water of the Pacific Ocean.) The hole is called an **impact** basin because it was probably made by an impact, or collision, with an asteroid or a comet. In the middle of the impact basin stands a tall cone that looks like a geyser or a volcano. Because Vesta is missing such a large chunk of land, it is shaped like a flattened football with a geyserlike nozzle.

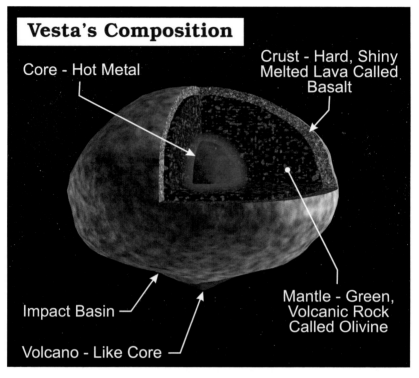

Vesta's Composition

Core - Hot Metal

Crust - Hard, Shiny Melted Lava Called Basalt

Impact Basin

Volcano - Like Core

Mantle - Green, Volcanic Rock Called Olivine

Vesta travels with a family of small asteroids, or meteoroids, that were chipped off when the giant basin was formed. These meteoroids also appear to be made from green olivine and dark lava. They travel near a zone where Jupiter's gravity can hurl them out of the asteroid belt and throw them into new orbits that cross Earth's orbit. When they land on Earth, these pieces of Vesta are known as a basaltic achondrite HED meteorites.

Ellemeet

On August 28, 1925, in the late morning, a stony meteorite from Vesta fell on the island of

Schouwen, part of the Netherlands. The meteorite broke into at least two pieces as it fell through the atmosphere. Witnesses saw a fireball and heard high-pitched screaming sounds in the sky that scared cows and horses in nearby meadows. After witnesses heard the sound of a large object crashing to Earth, they saw a dark cloud of dust rise in the midday sun.

One witness saw a small meteorite about four inches across and weighing about two pounds fall to Earth, where it made a hole about twenty inches deep. After it was dug up, the object fell into pieces. Later named the Ellemeet meteorite, this object contains a dark layer of carbonaceous chondrite, believed to be left over from a cometlike asteroid that collided with Vesta about 24 million years ago.

A light micrograph shows the detail of a carbonaceous chondrite meteorite.

The second piece of Vesta fell about a mile away. It weighed half a pound and made a hole about sixteen inches deep. This stone was left in the field, where it crumbled to dust within a year. A common occurrence for meteorites, many are never found because they bury themselves and crumble to dust. Some are preserved for many years, however, if they happen to land in hot deserts or cold, icy regions of Earth.

Moon Rocks

Although the meteorite in the Netherlands dissolved, others that land in extreme climates are preserved for many years. Lunar meteorites have been found in the hot Sahara Desert, where the lack of rain and hot climate helps preserve them. Many lunar meteorites have also been found in Antarctica. There, the icy conditions freeze the stones, allowing them to survive for thousands—or even millions—of years.

Some of the frozen meteorites found in Antarctica have a composition similar to rocks brought back from the moon between 1969 and 1972 by the Apollo space missions. Researchers think that these meteorites are pieces of the moon that broke off and fell to Earth.

These rocks were formed on the moon long ago when hot liquid rock shot up from lunar craters in a fountain of lava. Like water thrown

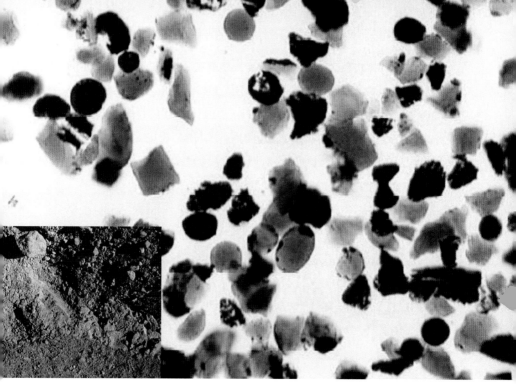

Apollo 17 astronauts collected orange and green lunar beads from the surface of the moon (inset photo).

through the air, the lava broke up into millions of liquid drops of hot, melted glassy rocks that cooled into solid glass beads and fell back on the ground.

The *Apollo 17* astronauts discovered this thick blanket of green and orange glass beads which formed a carpet of soil on the surface of the moon. And these amazing small glass beads have also been found in lunar meteorites.

ALH84001

Moon rocks, Earth rocks, and rocks from Mars are all shaped by the fire of volcanoes out of very similar materials. When meteors from the moon or from Mars land on Earth's rocky soil, they usually look very similar to all the other rocks. But Martian meteorite ALH84001 was easy to see. It stood out against the bright blue ice where it was discovered in the Allan Hills of Antarctica in 1984.

NASA scientists believe that ALH84001 was chipped off the surface of Mars by a meteoroid. Eventually this piece of the ancient Martian landscape found its way to Earth. Scientists found tiny fossils, minerals, and carbons in the meteorite, making some scientists think there may have once been life on Mars. Other scientists disagree, and a lively debate continues.

Water on Mars?

The surface of Mars is a dry and lifeless desert, baked by the hot sun. But scientists do not know what lies under the surface of the planet. Many scientists believe that Mars was once a lively world that looked a lot like Earth. They believe it once had rivers and oceans of water and a thick atmosphere to protect it from the burning sun.

Many scientists believe that Mars turned from a lovely garden into a dry, rusty colored cratered desert when it was bombarded by asteroids or comets. At this time, the Martian landscape appears to have many dried-up riverbeds and canyons carved by ancient rivers.

Martian meteorite ALH84001 (above), was found in Antarctica. Scientists have found (blue) microfossils inside the meteorite (bottom).

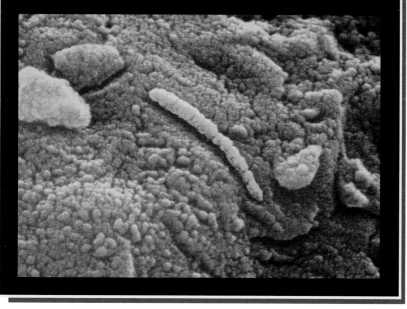

When Mars was bombarded, ALH84001 may have flown out of one of the ancient craters in the southern highlands. It is a piece of the red planet that dates back to the time when Mars may have had the kind of warm, wet environment needed to support life. For this reason, some scientists believe that the little fossils in ALH84001 are signs of ancient life on Mars.

Surprises in the Rocks

Many surprises are locked inside the volcanic rocks formed on other planets. Trapped in the melted glass of Martian meteorites, scientists found little bubbles that still contain gases from the ancient atmosphere of Mars. Like geodes that fly out of volcanoes on Earth, many space rocks are plain on the outside and filled with little gems on the inside. Rocks that look very ordinary may actually be visitors from outer space!

4

Metal Meteorites

Large planets and asteroids are made up of layers of materials. They have an outer crust made out of light rock, and under that a mantle, a layer of heavy melted volcanic rock. Because metal is a heavy element, it sinks down to the center of the planet to create the core. Usually, this metal stays deep within the planet or asteroid. But sometimes the large planets and asteroids crash into one another so hard that the inner metal core of the planet is exposed.

Iron meteorites come from the very core of parent bodies that were probably broken up in violent collisions that exposed their cores to more collisions. More than sixty different asteroids are made mostly of crystals of iron and nickel metal. They are fairly bright and bluish in color, and they orbit in the central regions of the main asteroid belt.

Kleopatra

On May 4, 2000, NASA astronomers collected the first radar images of an asteroid in the main asteroid belt. It was a metallic, dog bone–shaped rock the size of New Jersey, probably left over from a very old, violent collision. The asteroid, named 216 Kleopatra, is about 135 miles long and about 58 miles wide. Kleopatra was discovered in 1880, but its shape was unknown until 2000.

Several views of the dog bone-shaped asteroid 216 Kleopatra, which is the size of New Jersey.

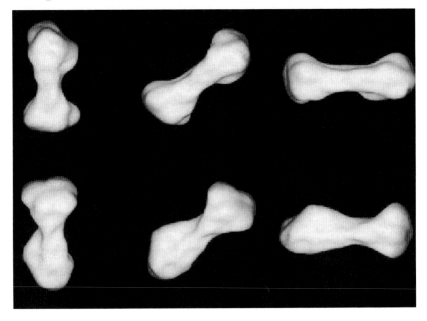

The surface of Kleopatra is made of loose, porous metal rubble. The odd-shaped asteroid has two globe-shaped ends connected by a handle, like a dumbbell or dog bone. Astronomers believe that Kleopatra may have once been two separate globes in orbit around each other with empty space between them. Many asteroids have companions that orbit around each other, either as a pair of separate globes, or as globes gently fused together.

Though Kleopatra's amazing shape has puzzled astronomers over the mystery of asteroid collisions, astronomers do not believe the metal asteroid will ever hit Earth. But violent metal asteroid collisions have launched meteoroids that eventually did collide with Earth.

Artist P.I. Medvedev was one of the few people to ever see such an event. He was sitting at his window in the town of Iman in Russia when an iron meteorite fell. (He made a painting of the event, which was reproduced as a Russian postage stamp to commemorate the tenth anniversary of the event in 1957.)

Sikhote-Alin

The Sikhote-Alin iron meteorite fell at 10:38 in the morning on February 12, 1947. Witnesses saw a flaming red fireball changing to other colors as it fell. It was brighter than the morning

Artwork depicts the Sikhote-Alin iron meteorite crashing outside a village in eastern Siberia.

sun, shedding sparks and casting a moving shadow on the ground. It rained a shower of fireballs into the thick forest on the Sikhote-Alin Mountains in eastern Siberia.

About one thousand tons of metallic rock fell from the sky, leaving a trail of swirling smoke and dust twenty miles long that lingered in the sky for several hours. About four miles above the mountains, the meteorite exploded into thousands of pieces. The huge explosion was seen and heard two hundreds miles away and felt more than one hundred miles away.

When the main mass exploded, pieces of meteorite blasted in every direction. Meteorites were even found embedded in nearby trees. Some pieces were steel-blue, with their surface melted into thumb print shapes during their fall. Some were sharp and jagged, because they were torn apart by a violent explosion only three-and-a-half miles above the ground. Some looked like a falling raindrop, with a tail of burning metal frozen in time.

Clearings were blasted open in the thick forest, which is home to Siberian tigers and brown bears. In the clearings, there were more than one hundred impact craters, bowl-shaped holes with flat floors and uplifted centers. The

A fragment of the Sikhote-Alin meteorite found in the mountains of Siberia.

largest impact crater was twenty feet deep and eighty-five feet across. An iron meteorite weighing about two tons was found inside. Such giant iron meteorites have played an important role in human history.

The Iron Age

In the Stone Age, humans made tools from bone, wood, and stone. Later, humans found copper and bronze to make better tools, and the Bronze Age began. Then around 1400 B.C., iron was found to make even better tools. Early humans used the iron ores that fell from the sky as meteorites. Early toolmakers called this marvelous metal by names such as fire from heaven and thunderbolt of heaven.

An iron dagger made from a meteorite was found in the tomb of the fourteenth-century B.C. Egyptian pharaoh Tutankhamen. Meanwhile in Greenland, native Inuits made carving tools, knives, and fishing harpoons from iron meteorites. Ancient traders took these tools as far as fourteen hundred miles away. In 1818 British explorer Captain John Ross met the Inuit in Greenland. They showed him their iron tools and told him the iron came from a mountain with a huge iron rock in it.

For seventy-five years explorers looked for the meteorite, but the Inuit would not tell them where to find their iron from heaven. Then, in

1894, explorer Robert Peary persuaded a local guide to bring him there. He was amazed to discover three giant iron meteorites, which the Inuit had named "the tent," "the woman," and "the dog."

Explorer Robert Peary prepares to journey in search of the coveted "iron from heaven."

"The tent" weighed thirty-four tons. About half of "the woman" had been chipped away, leaving twenty-one tons. "The dog" was the smallest, at eleven hundred pounds. Peary's team shipped the giant iron meteorites to New York City and sold them to the American Museum of Natural History for $40,000. He used the money to pay for his famous trip to the North Pole. Metal from meteorites has long been a source for many kinds of discoveries and riches.

The Sudbury Star Wound

Almost 2 billion years ago, one of the largest meteorites to ever strike Earth created a huge basin in Sudbury in Ontario, Canada. The asteroid was about five-and-a-half miles wide, about the size of Mount Everest. The giant hole it made is known as an **astrobleme**, which means "star wound" in the Greek language.

Metals from the ancient meteorite have made Sudbury one of the richest mining regions in the world. About 8 million tons each of nickel and copper have been mined there, as well as smaller amounts of platinum, palladium, cobalt, iron, sulfur, gold, silver, selenium, tellurium, and many other metals and minerals.

Besides a great variety of metals and minerals, Fullerines, also know as buckyballs, have also been found in the *astrobleme*. They are named after architect Buckminster Fuller because they look like the **geodesic domes** he designed. Buckyballs are made of carbon atoms linked together in the shape of a soccer ball. Instead of air, the tiny hollow buckyballs are filled with gases such as helium and argon from outer space. Buckyballs have been found in carbon-type asteroids and comets, such as the Murchison meteorite.

Because of its roundness, a buckyball can bounce back from a fifteen thousand miles per

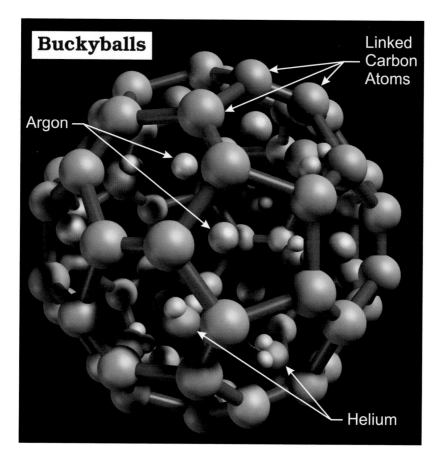

Buckyballs

Linked Carbon Atoms

Argon

Helium

hour collision with a steel plate. When it is compressed, a buckyball can be made into a diamond more than twice as hard as a diamond from Earth. Scientists have not been able to melt a buckyball. Buckyballs may have been formed inside red giants (carbon stars) at least 5 billion years ago, and were later swept in to help form the solar system.

A Connection to the Universe

Before the buckyball was discovered in 1985, there were only two kinds of carbon known to exist on Earth—graphite and compressed graphite, known as diamonds. All the life forms on Earth, including the plants and the animals, are carbon-based life forms.

Meteorites contain some of the most fascinating materials on the planet. They remind us of our connection to the whole universe, including the stars in the sky. When the stars fall to Earth as meteors, they bring with them many wonderful things to discover about life and the universe.

Glossary

asteroid: A small planetlike object that revolves around the sun, usually in the main asteroid belt between Jupiter and Mars.

astrobleme: A very large, oval-shaped crater created by a giant meteorite.

basin: A large, bowl-shaped hole in the surface of the land or ocean floor.

comet: A loosely packed ball of carbon dust, filled with ice and gas that jets out into a tail when its long oval orbit brings it close to the sun.

constellation: A group of stars that are seen as a figure or design in the sky.

ejected: Thrown out forcefully.

friction: The rubbing of one surface or object against another.

geodesic dome: A rounded structure made of straight flat forms that lock together.

impact: The force or effect of one body hitting another.

meteor: A bright tail that appears in the sky when the friction of a falling meteoroid heats up Earth's atmosphere.

meteorite: A piece of carbon, stone, or metal that has fallen to Earth from outer space.

meteoroid: A solid body moving in space, which is smaller than an asteroid and at least as large as a speck of dust.

orbit: The path of one body moving around another in space.

For Further Exploration

Billy Aronson, *Meteors: The Truth Behind Shooting Stars*. New York: Franklin Watts, 1996. Explains the difference between a meteor, a meteoroid, and a meteorite, and what happens when an asteroid or comet gets too close to Earth.

Isaac Asimov, *Comets and Meteors*. Milwaukee: G. Stevens Children's Books, 1990. Discusses comets and meteors, including famous appearances and unexplained mysteries connected with them.

Fred Bortz, *Martian Fossils on Earth?: The Story of Meteorite ALH 84001*. Brookfield, CT: Millbrook Press, 1997. Discusses the study of a meteorite found in Antarctica in 1984 and why it is thought to have come from Mars.

Franklyn Mansfield Branley, *Shooting Stars* New York: Crowell, 1989. Explains what shooting stars are made of and what happens to them when they land on Earth.

Roy A. Gallant, *Comets, Asteroids, and Meteorites.* Tarrytown, NY: Benchmark Books, 2001. An introduction to asteroids, meteoroids and meteorites, and comets.

Robin Kerrod, *Asteroids, Comets, and Meteors.* Minneapolis: Lerner Publications, 2000. Introduces asteroids, comets, and meteors. Discusses where they came from, what they are made of, their orbits, and what effect they have on Earth and other bodies in the solar system.

Paul P. Sipiera, *Comets and Meteor Showers.* New York: Childrens Press, 1997. Introduction to comets, covering where they come from, how they travel, and their relationship to meteor showers.

Gregory L. Vogt, *Asteroids, Comets, and Meteors.* Brookfield, CT: Milbrook Press, 1996. Discusses asteroids, comets, and meteors, and what scientists learned when a comet hit Jupiter.

Index

gas planets, 5–6
Geminids, 11–12

Halley's comet, 10

Iman, Russia, 35
Inuit, 38–40
Iron Age, 38
iron meteorites, 33–34

Johnson Space Center, 18, 20
Jupiter, 13–15

Kleopatra (asteroid), 34–35

Leonids, 10–11

Mars, 25, 29–30, 32
Medvedev, P.I., 35
metals
  in asteroids, 33–34
  in Kleopatra asteroid, 34–35
  in meteorites, 30–40
meteor dust, 6–7, 9
meteorites
  ALH84001, 29–30, 32
  basaltic achondrite HED, 26
  buckyballs in, 41
  carbon, 16–18, 19, 20–22, 23
  colors of, 35
  composition of, 23
  Ellemeet, 26–27
  falls described, 17–18
  formation of, 13
  iron, 33–34
  lunar, 28–29
  metals in, 30–40
  Monahans, 18, 20
  Murchison, 18, 19, 41
  preservation of, 28
  Sikhote-Alin, 35–38
  Sudbury, 40
  Sudbury metal, 40
  Yukon Falls, 20–22
meteoroids, 6–7, 9, 13
meteors
  colors of, 11
  formation of, 9
  showers, 9–10, 11–12
  storms, 10–11
Monahans, Texas, 18, 20
moon

of Jupiter, 14
rocks from, 25, 28–29
Murchison, Australia, 18, 19, 41

name, 4
nickel, 34

Ontario, Canada, 40
orbits
  of asteroid companions, 35
  of comets, 6
  of meteoroids, 13
  of Vesta, 26
Orion, 9
Orionids, 9, 10

Peary, Robert, 39–40
Perseids, 9–10
Phaeton (asteroid), 11
planets
  baby, 16–17
  composition of, 33
  formation of, 5–6

Ross, John, 38

Sahara Desert, 28
salt, 20
Siberia, 36
Sikhote-Alin (meteorite), 35–38
solar system
  formation of, 4–6, 20
  Jupiter as mini, 13–15
Stone Age, 38
stony asteroids, 23–25
Sudbury Star wound, 40
Swift-Tuttle comet, 9–10

tails
  asteroids and, 16
  of comets, 6, 11
Tutankhamen (Egyptian
  pharaoh), 38

Vesta (asteroid), 25–26, 27, 28

water
  in carbon asteroids, 15–16
  in carbon meteorites, 18, 20, 23
  on Mars, 30, 32

Yukon Falls, Canada, 20–22